BOOK FOR YOU

FROM :

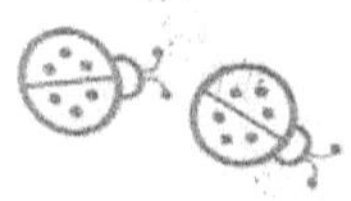

Little Missy Helper:

Be Kind Be Helpful

For Kids of All Ages

ISBN: 9781068817700

eBook: 9781068817717

Interior and Cover Artwork: Jessie Eldora Photography

Jessie Eldora Robertson

Little Missy Helper:

Be Kind Be Helpful

For Kids of All Ages

ISBN: 9781068817700

eBook: 9781068817717

Interior and Cover Artwork: Jessie Eldora Photography

Jessie Eldora Robertson

Prologue/Introduction:

When I first thought of writing this story; I thought it was
a 'no go'. I was still on heavy pain killer pills, and not long out
of the hospital. Thinking it would be an unhappy book.
I left it there.
But, later on seeing how helpful a 6-year-old can be,
I picked up the pen. This little great granddaughter inspired me
to write.

Quotes from – You Come Too – Robert Frost –
Favorite Poems for Young Readers.
{Dedication: To Belle Moodie Frost, how knew as a teacher
that no poetry was good for children that wasn't equally good for
their elders.}
Forward: Hyde Cox: "Something there is that doesn't love a wall."
One of the meanings I could give it that the poet has never added
a single stone to the wall that so often separates age from youth.
Synopsis:

A little girl turns 6 years old and has the experience of seeing
her great grammy fall. She never had an occasion where someone
had to be rushed by ambulance to another city. She watches the
progress of her grandmother's healing, which is about 6 months.
She is automatically helpful and loving to her grammy.
This is a different venture for little Aria.
Addition: a second kids' fun story - Zippy and Other
Stuffie Friends. Can a mouse be part of the Stuffie family?

Synopsis:

A little girl turns 6 years old and has the experience of seeing her great grammy fall. She never had an occasion where someone had to be rushed by ambulance to another city. She watches the progress of her grandmother's healing, which is about 6 months. She is automatically helpful and loving to her grammy. This is a different venture for little Aria.

I dedicate this story book to my husband Bill

He waited on me, and took pictures while I

was healing ... and he learned how to Child-proof

the home.

My Great Grammy is getting to what
used to be

She can walk straight now, today

Walking tall even if she is a shortie,

Healing from a broken hip, a fall a
display,

Such a frailty

The accident happened on my 6th
Birthday

No one ate the cake, being it was too
late,

Grammy tripped on a lamp cord lay

She lay still, didn't move, it was bad
fate

I opened my gifts late

Grammy doesn't need her wheelchair

Everyone is making it easier

She got rid of her long hair

Everyone is pleasing her

Trying to ...

It is spring, warm and sunny

Grammy looks out the window

The white-tail deer, jump quickly

I think one is a doe

A nuance and a beauty

Grammy is in slow movement

She is shaky and can't pick-up ...

My toys or anything to improvement

She drops her pills and knitting, yuck

Patience needed

I cuddle with my Grammy still

Warmly, sharing her heating pad

My stuffies and my blanky, and her pill,

I bring my computer tablet pad

We play the games

Christmas baking time

Papa teaches me a little bit by bit

I'm doing just fine

For being 6,

I'm a big hit

Pa pa is a good baker

I am trying to learn, like the book

When I grow up, I may be a taker

I want to be a good cook

I want to be a Chef like Pa pa

Mommy is baking today

Cake making, I am looking only

All the way

Smacking my lips, that's not baloney

I eat the icing and then the cake

Swing up 1, swing to close

Steady now grammy, don't lose your
balance

I'll help you with your pose

Exercises to get you strong allowance

So, you can go outside

Can't wear those pretty Philippine flips

At least not too soon

Can't risk falling down, keep your grip

Be careful now, don't dare swoon

I'll get your cane

I'll stay close by, to help aide

You can't put your one sock on

With your new slip-in shoes laid

Your muscles seem to be gone

Pray for Blessings ☺

What a warm and cuddly thing

Sitting prettily, granddaughter,

 great granddaughter,

And grammy in the big swing

That's the way its otter ... be

We are so loved

I had fun with the ramp inside

My cars and trucks loved moving up
and down

My toys are all scattered beside the
ride

But grammy made a frown

She can't get to her computer desk ...
not helpful me

Dear God,

Listen to me, now!

Grammy needs a Healing touch

Grammy needs help

in her con-val-les-sance

Bless this home I pray

It's me Aria ...

Thank you ... and please

Zippy

and

Other

Stuffie

Friends

It's a snowing and wintery day

Papa is shoveling snow against the home boarder skirt,

Mice are out to hide, "hey!"

Aria guesses that is why Papa does exsert,

To do so much work!

Was that a mouse?

Mice are fastest, like a bird on a branch

I saw it but ... it flew south

A mouse, not sure ... couldn't see ... no chance

Glad it is out of my bedroom, I think?

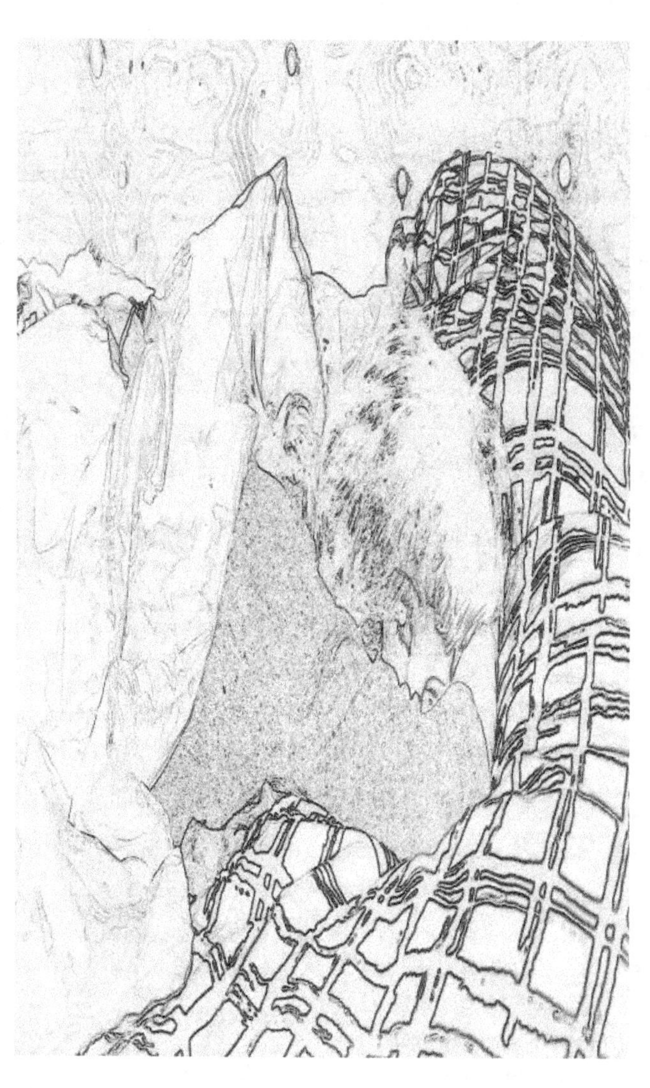

Ooh, what's that I feel on my face ...

In the quiet of the night,

I did feel 'something' race!

Coming from my cozy squared pillows so light

Mommy said, "**don't** bring food into the bedroom!"

Grammy is knitting my dolly a dress

She keeps her holey socks in the box

Until she can do her darndest best

But what does Grammy find a lot,

Seeds scattered everywhere? Seeds?

Two fluffiest new mouse stuffies,

Two, to snuggle with, for Aria's nap

She would like more mouse lovelies,

With cute ears and eyes in her lap

Aria has doggies, kitties, squish-

melons and more ...

Mom says no **rodent** mice!

It all started with Oobert

The Teddy bear who went to bed,

This stuffy was just too soft and cute,

Every night sleeps with Aria it's said

Of course, sharing with Blue Blankie

Aria likes cuddling and playing with

Mama stuffy, a smore

And baby Patty-cake, that is a pancake

The newest thing ... food stuffies, add more

The two new can relate

Keeping cool under the air conditioner

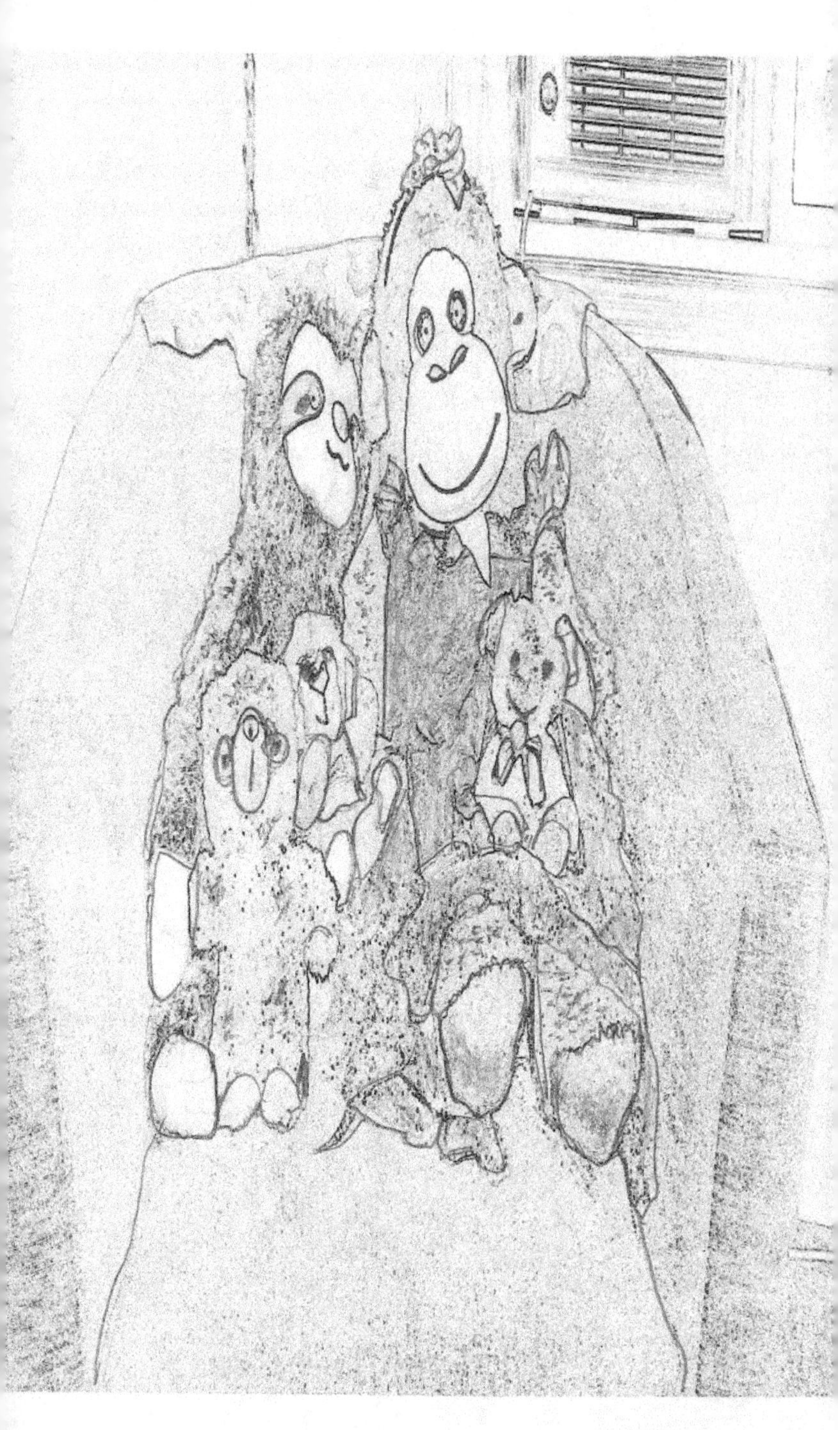

Aria likes to play 'Family,'

A big stuffie animal family portrait

Big Monkey the largest is the father,

But he gets to wear Aria's princess
outfit

The little bears wear their fur

'n Slough too

One day Nanook licked yogurt up

Licked-it-up from Aria's hand,

He's a real animal too, a dog, yup

He lives on Auntie Leah's farmland

Aria can't **keep**, but she can visit!

And, then there's Scully the cat

Can he chase the mice away on a visit?

Wooden boat made by Grandpa

Sailing mastered by Aria in low water

The snail shells are what she saw

Collecting the fancy rocks in water

No stuffies to the lake water!

The day came for a big surprise!

Something orange and in glass

A goldfish, an animal pet, alive!

It is for Aria on her Birthday, at last

Aria is so happy! And happy to be 7!

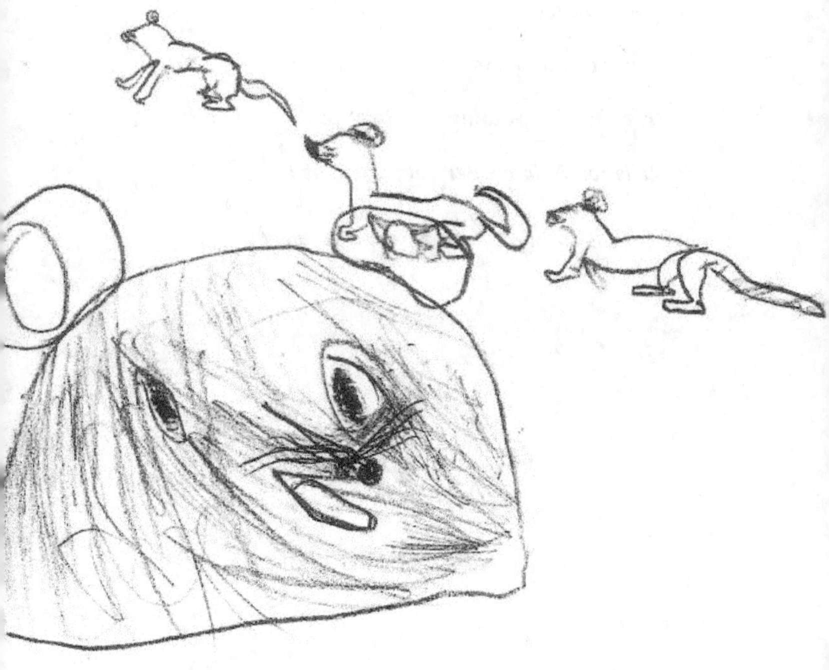

Was there 1 Mouse?

The Answer is 4
2 Mice

The author lives in the Cariboo Chilcotin in Williams Lake, BC., with her husband Bill, and her granddaughter & great granddaughter. She is a self-taught, a self-starter in many of her talents.

The author was born and raised in Prince George, British Columbia, Canada.

As an Illustrator and Photographer:

The Author comes by her artistic albitites, being a natural, as were her mother and aunt. Jessie's creativity comes from been given a sewing machine and a camera at a very young age. Jessie has traveled Cross Canada taking photographs all the way. Her photos are shown in her memoir, Working Like A Man – Revised *. Photographs also in the book, The Autobody Repair Man – Memoir, by George L. Phillips. Jessie has illustrated her children's book and Audio book, Run Away and Hide: Hiding. The latest published book is: From Where Grandma Sits: Birdwatching – Little Missy Foodie, a series to (above) Run Away and Hide. Jessie is published in Online photography sites: Shutterstock, Getty Images/istock and Dreamstime. Published writing includes Anthologies in poetry books.

Other books by the Author

Run Away and Hide: Hiding – Young children's book.
 *Available in Audio.

Little Missy Foodie – Children's book – ages 3 – 8.

From Where Grandma Sits: Birdwatching – for kids of all ages.
May 2024.

Working Like A Man * Best Edition: Memoir
* Nominated for Eric Hoffer Book Awards - 2024

Books edited & illustrated by the author,
 Jessie Eldora Robertson:
The Autobody Repair Man: Memoir by George L. Phillips

-    All books available on Amazon.

Imprint of: Lake Nest Publishing
Art credit – on Mouse Artwork on the Title page of
Zippy and Other Stuffies Friends: by Aria
Also, Mice Artwork on page 61, by Aria

9 798230 596967